# Introduction

The old adage "practice makes perfect" can really hold true for a ch[illegible]ucation. The more practice and exposure a child has to concepts being taught in school, the more success they are likely to find. For many parents, knowing how to best support their child's learning can be frustrating. This book is designed to eliminate the guesswork for parents using it at home and also be a valuable resource for educators using it in the classroom. It provides practical support for children and educators alike.

*Here's how:* As young learners begin to read, they need to learn to connect the letters they see to the sounds they hear. Making this connection is a crucial step toward becoming fluent readers. It provides the foundation for future reading and spelling skills.

*Practice Makes Perfect: Phonics (K–1)* covers the following skills:

- sound recognition
- relationships between letters and sounds
- short vowel sounds
- short vowel word families
- long vowel sounds and common spelling patterns
- beginning consonant blends
- beginning digraphs

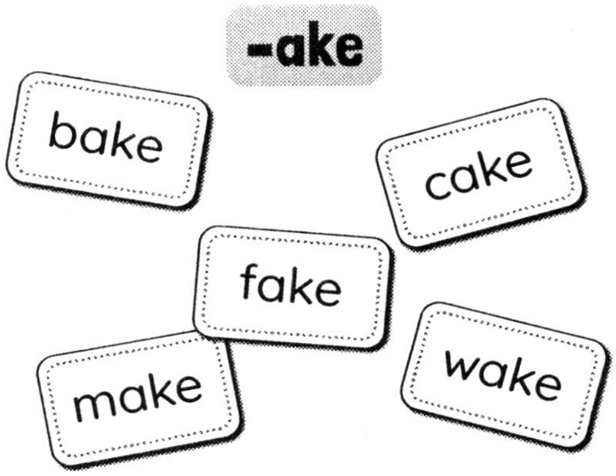


## Inside This Resource

**Practice Pages**—The 43 practice pages (pages 4–46) are organized sequentially so that children can build their knowledge from letter formation and individual letter sounds to short-vowel and long-vowel word families. Common blends and digraphs are introduced to complete the practice pages provided.

**Answer Key**—This comprehensive key (pages 47–48) provides the answers for each practice page.

## Helpful Tips

- Keep practice sessions short, positive, and constructive.
- Help with instructions. Consider asking your child to repeat what they are being asked to do for each practice page.
- Look for ways to encourage your child to use the words and skills they are learning in their everyday lives by reading signs, books, and other print items around them.
- Make flash cards or lists of words that your child struggles with. Provide additional practice with these words for a few minutes each day.
- Read to your child every day. Encourage your child to read words they know in the book, or take turns reading pages of the book.

**Practice 1**

*Initial Sounds b & c*

Name: ______________________________

**Directions:** Name each picture and listen to the beginning sounds. Color the pictures that begin with the **b** sound.

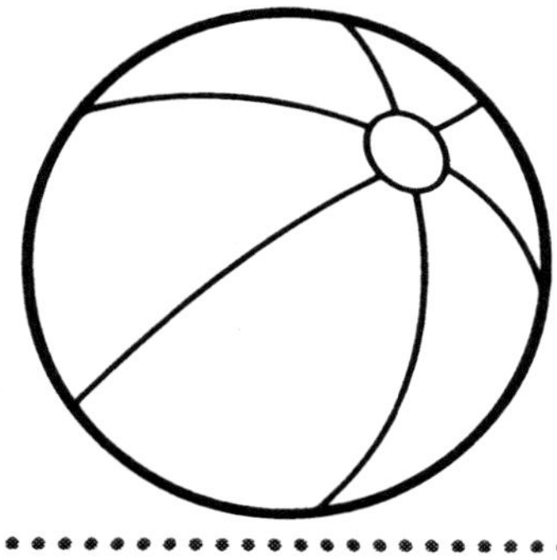

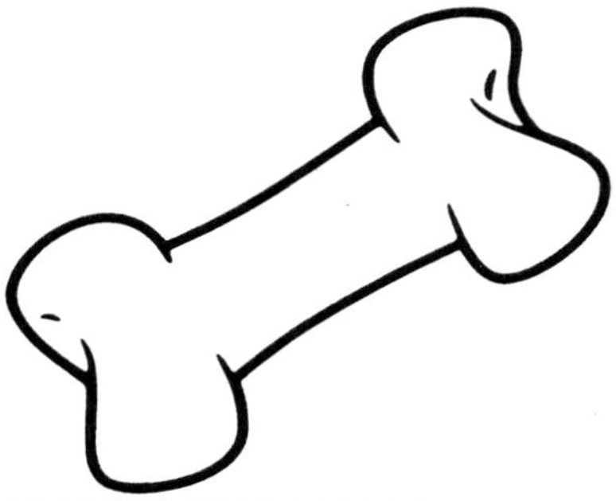

**Directions:** Add the letter **c** to the beginning of each group of letters. Then read each word.

____at

____ow

____up

____an

GRADES K-1

Practice MAKES PERFECT

# Phonics

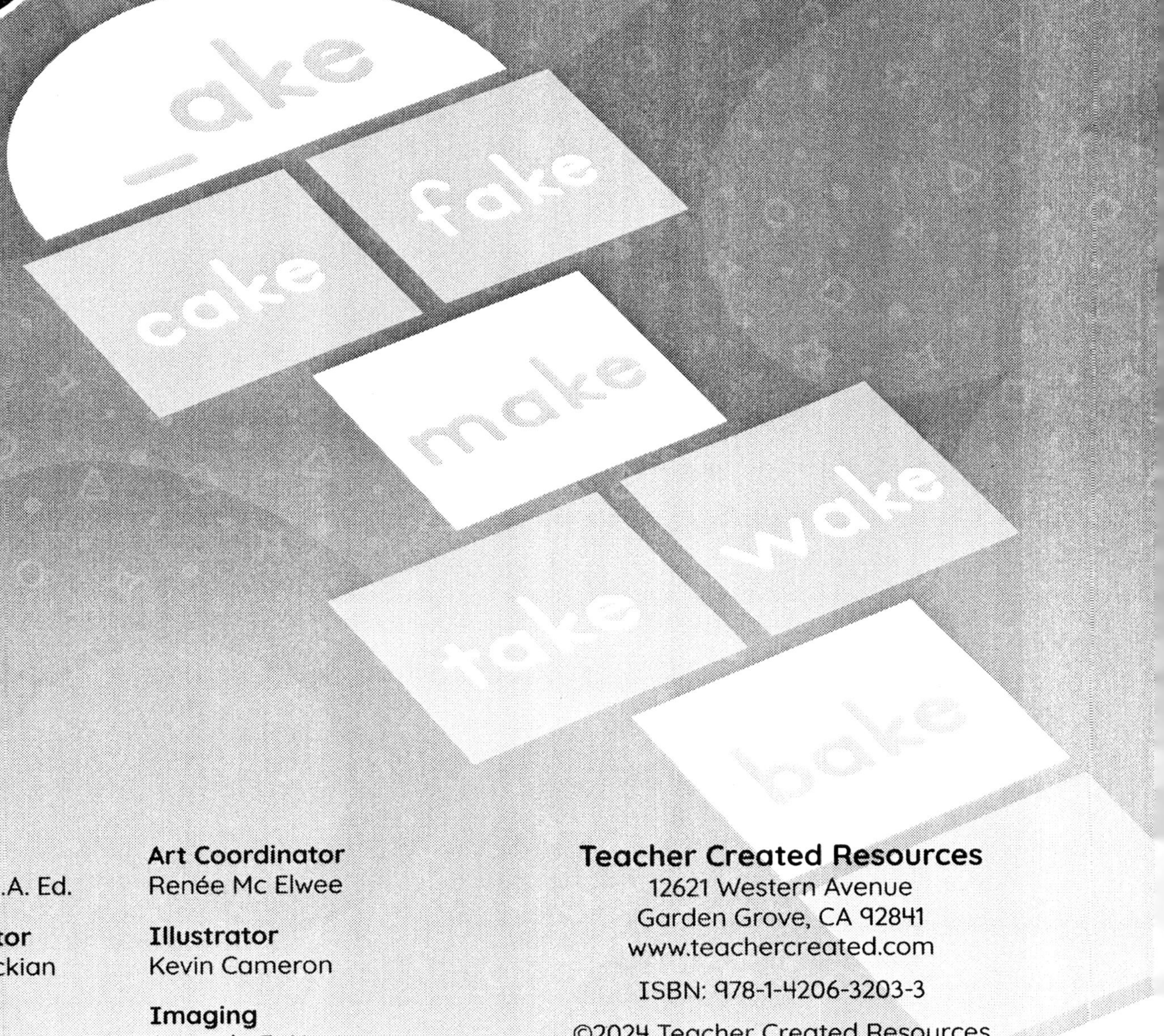



**Author**
Kristy Stark, M.A. Ed.

**Managing Editor**
Mara Ellen Guckian

**Editor in Chief**
Brent L. Fox, M. Ed.

**Creative Director**
Sarah M. Fournier

**Cover Artist**
Diem Pascarella

**Art Coordinator**
Renée Mc Elwee

**Illustrator**
Kevin Cameron

**Imaging**
Amanda R. Harter

**Publisher**
Mary D. Smith, M.S. Ed.



**Teacher Created Resources**
12621 Western Avenue
Garden Grove, CA 92841
www.teachercreated.com

ISBN: 978-1-4206-3203-3



©2024 Teacher Created Resources



Reprinted, 2024

Made in U.S.A.

For standards correlations, visit
*http://www.teachercreated.com/standards/*

Teacher Created Resources



The classroom teacher may reproduce the materials in this book for use in a single classroom only. The reproduction of any part of this book for other classrooms or for an entire school or school system is strictly prohibited. No part of this publication may be transmitted or recorded in any form without written permission from the publisher.

# Table of Contents

Name: ______________________________

**Directions:** Listen to the beginning sound of each picture. Add a **d** or an **f** to complete each word.

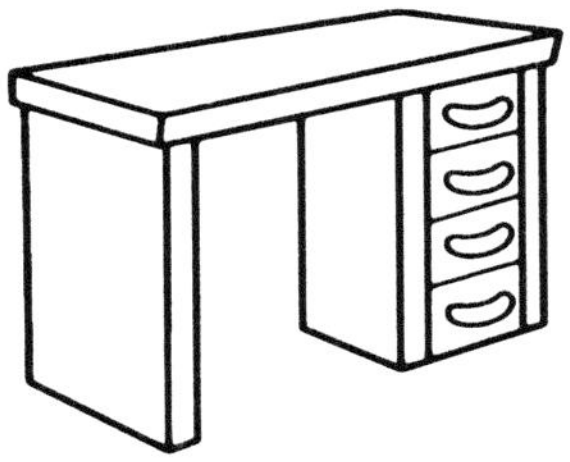
___esk

___an

___og

___ip

___ig

___ish

___rog

___ox

**Directions:** Use the words above that begin with **d** or **f** to complete the sentences below.

**1.** We have two ______________________.

**2.** The duck is on the ______________________!

**3.** That ______________ can ______________!

**4.** A ______________ is by the ______________.

**Practice 3**

*Initial Sounds*
*g & h*

Name: ______________________________

**Directions:** Name each picture and listen to the beginning sounds. Color the pictures that begin with the **g** sound.

**Directions:** Add the letter **h** to the beginning of each group of letters. Then read each word.

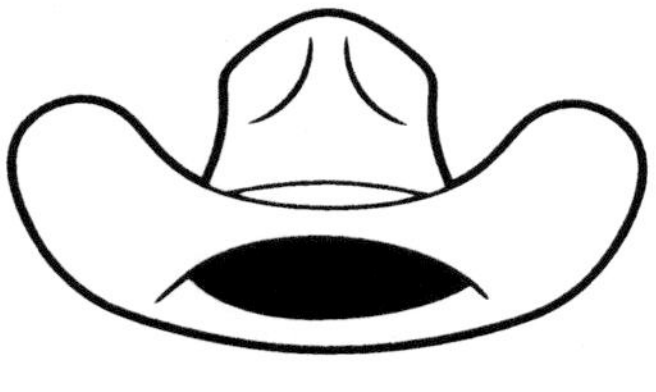

____at

____ill

____and

____ome

Practice 4
*Initial Sounds*
*j & k*

Name: ______________________________

**Directions:** Listen to the beginning sound of each picture. Add a **j** or a **k** to complete each word.

   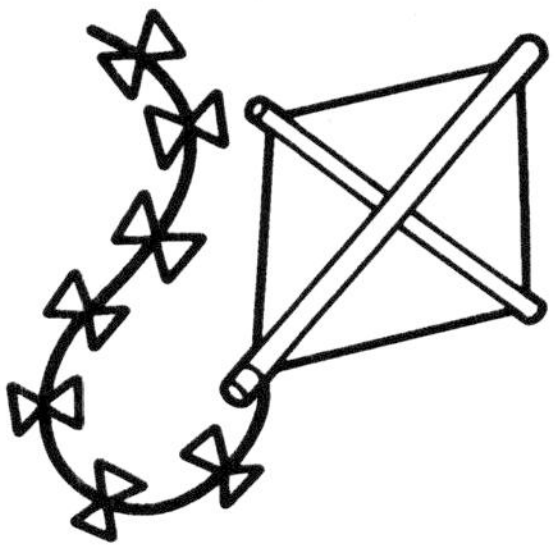

____et ____ey ____ug ____ite

____ar ____ump ____ing ____ick

**Directions:** Use the words above that begin with **j** or **k** to complete the sentences below.

**1.** Put the bugs in the ______________________.

**2.** He can ______________________ the ball far.

**3.** The ________________ has a ________________.

Practice 5
*Initial Sounds*
*l & m*

Name: ______________________________

**Directions:** Name each picture and listen to the beginning sounds. Color the pictures that begin with the **l** sound.

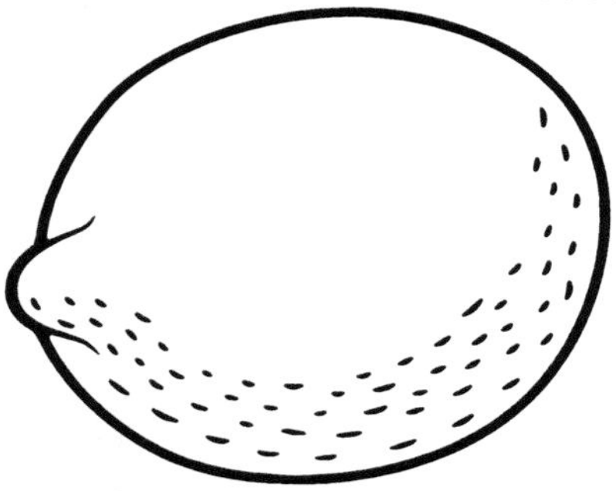

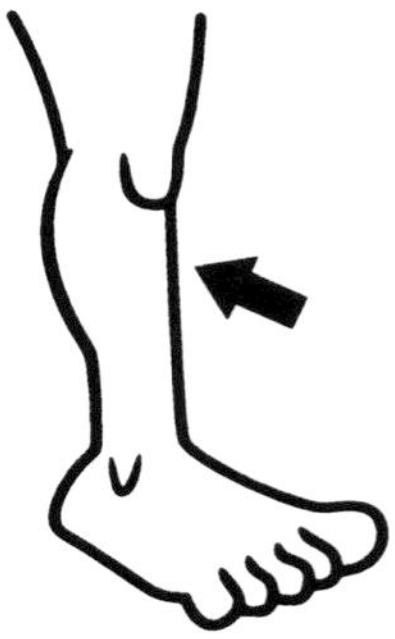

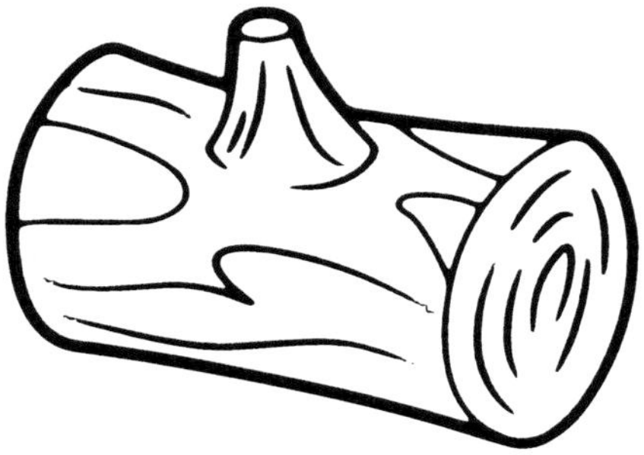

**Directions:** Add the letter **m** to the beginning of each group of letters. Then read each word.

___op

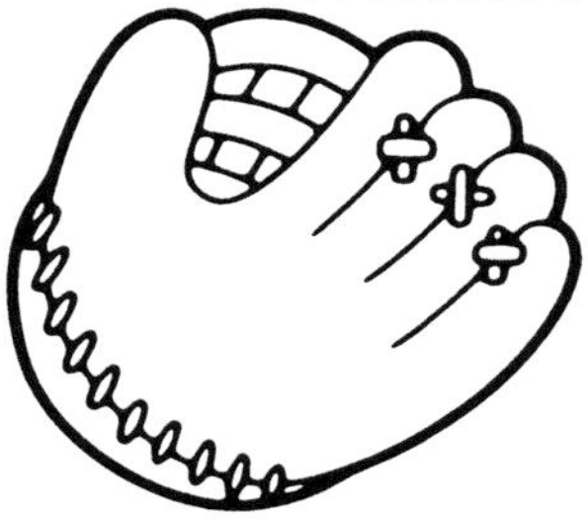

___itt

___ug

___ap

Name: ______________________________

**Directions:** Listen to the beginning sound of each picture. Add an **n** or a **p** to complete each word.

___ig

___ail

___lum

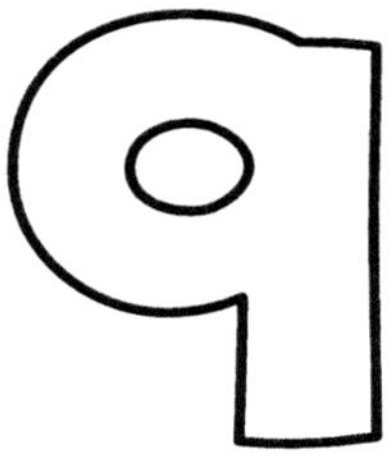
___ine

___in

___est

___ut

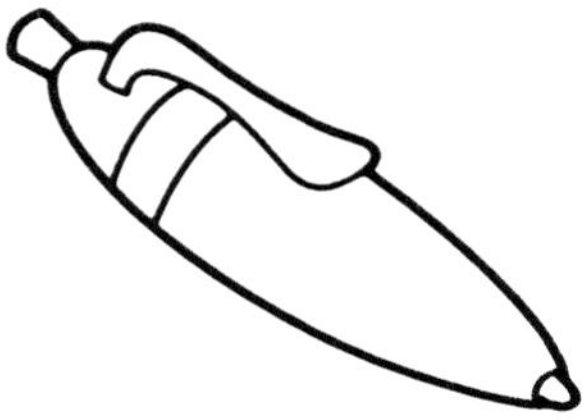
___en

**Directions:** Use the words above that begin with **n** or **p** to complete the sentences below.

**1.** The bird made a ______________________________.

**2.** One ______________________________ fell out.

**3.** The ______________________________ likes to play.

**4.** This is the number ______________________________.

**Practice 7**
*Initial Sounds*
*q & r*

Name: ____________________________________________

**Directions:** Name each picture and listen to the beginning sounds. Color the pictures that begin with the **q** sound.

**Directions:** Add the letter **r** to the beginning of each group of letters. Then read each word.

____ake

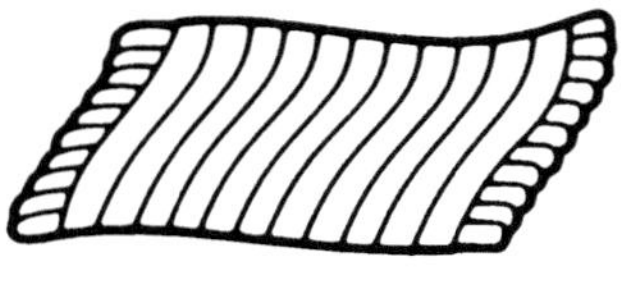

____ug

____ing

____am


©Teacher Created Resources

Name: ______________________________

**Directions:** Listen to the beginning sound of each picture. Add an **s** or a **t** to complete each word.

___ix

___ape

___un

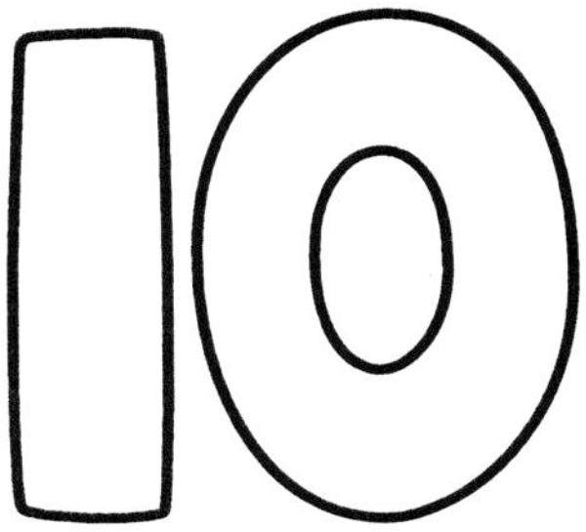
___en

___tar

___ruck

___ock

___ent

**Directions:** Use the words above that begin with **s** or **t** to complete the sentences below.

**1.** A six is on the ______________________.

**2.** The number ten is on that ______________________.

**3.** He has a ______________________ on one sock.

Name: ______________________________

**Directions:** Name each picture and listen to the beginning sounds. Color the pictures that begin with the **v** sound.

**Directions:** Add the letter **w** to the beginning of each group of letters. Then read each word.

____eb

____ell

____atch

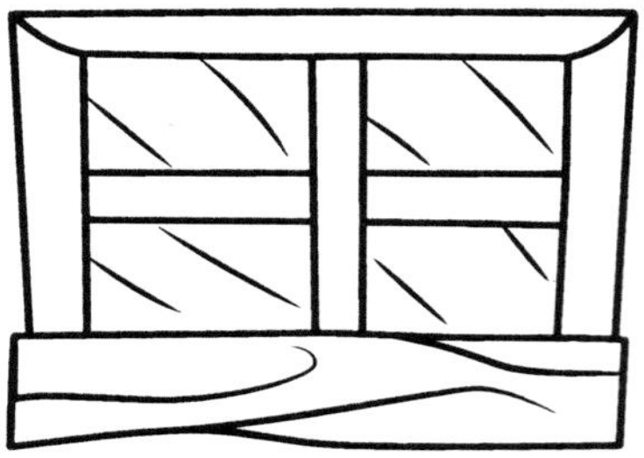
____indow

 ©Teacher Created Resources

Name: ____________________________________________

**Directions:** Listen to the beginning sound of each picture. Add a **y** or a **z** to complete each word.

___ebra ___arn ___ell ___ip

 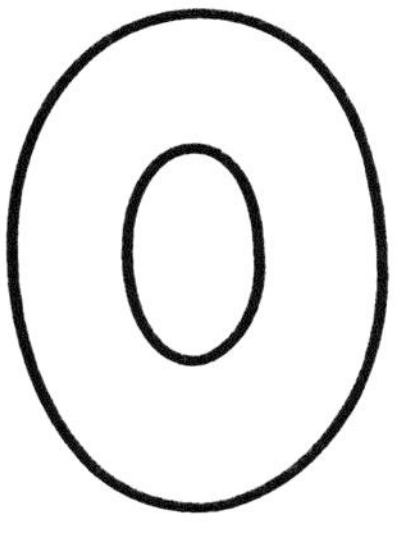 

___oo ___ak ___ero ___o-yo

**Directions:** Use the words above that begin with **y** or **z** to complete the sentences below.

**1.** That is a lot of ______________________________!

**2.** He can ______________________________ the zipper.

**3.** There are ______________________ eggs in the nest.

Name: ______________________________

**Directions:** Read each **-am** and **-ap** word and write it beside its picture. Then read the words in each word family and listen to the matching endings.

cap ham jam map nap ram

| **-am** | | **-ap** | |
|---|---|---|---|
|  | ______________ |  | ______________ |
|  | ______________ |  | ______________ |
|  | ______________ |  | ______________ |

**Directions:** Use words from the **-am** and **-ap** word families to complete the sentences below.

**1.** Pam likes ______________ but not ______________.

**2.** Sam is on a big ______________________!

**3.** It will be fun to use the ______________________.

 *©Teacher Created Resources*

Name: ______________________________

**Directions:** Draw lines to match each **-an** and **-at** word to its picture.

bat van pan cat

can hat man rat

**Directions:** Write the **-at** and **-an** words from above in the correct section below. Then read the words in each word family.

| **-an** | | **-at** | |
|---|---|---|---|
| ________ | ________ | ________ | ________ |
| ________ | ________ | ________ | ________ |

Name: ______________________________

**Directions:** Use the word wheels to make words for the **-et** and **-en** word families. Write the words on the lines and read the words in each word family. The first ones have been done for you.

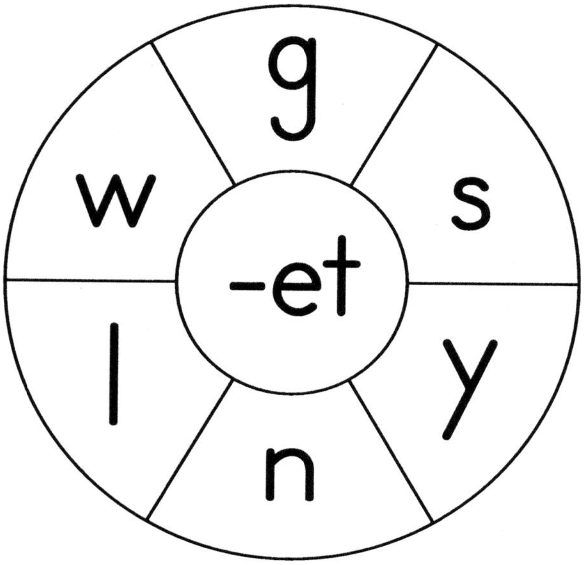


**-et**

get ____________

____________ ____________

____________ ____________

**-en**

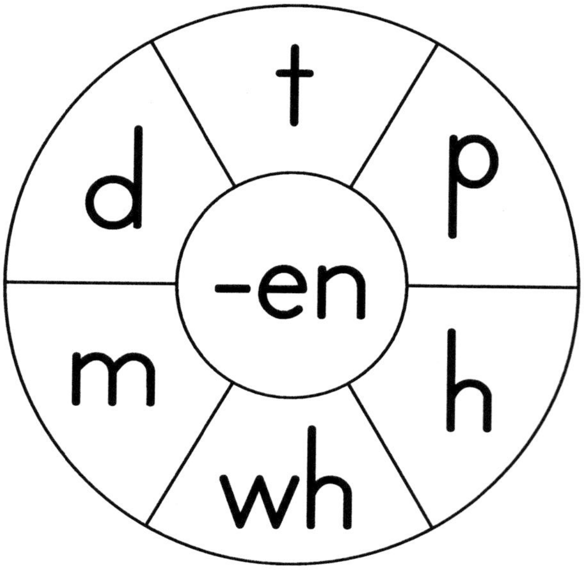


ten ____________

____________ ____________

____________ ____________

 ©Teacher Created Resources

Name: ______________________________

**Directions:** Name each picture and write the correct word family ending, **-est** or **-ell**. Then count the words in each word family and write the numbers in the boxes.

**-est words** ☐ **-ell words** ☐

b________

n________

y________

w________

sh________

v________

sm________

t________

r________

**Practice 15**
*Short I Word Families*
*-ig & -in*

Name: ______________________________

**Directions:** Read each **-ig** and **-in** word and write it under its picture. Then circle the **-ig** words in red and circle the **-in** words in blue. Read the words in each word family.

bin chin fin grin pig pin twig wig

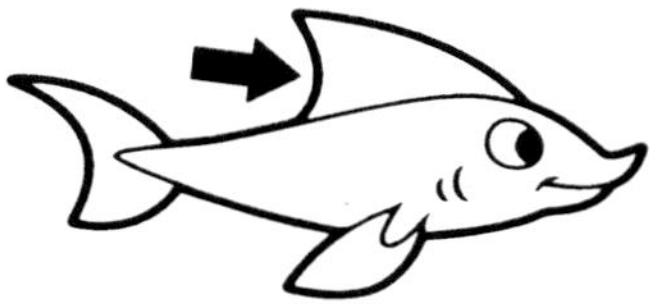

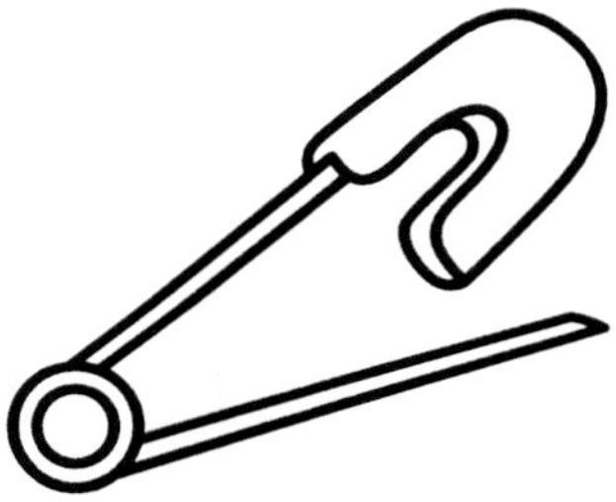
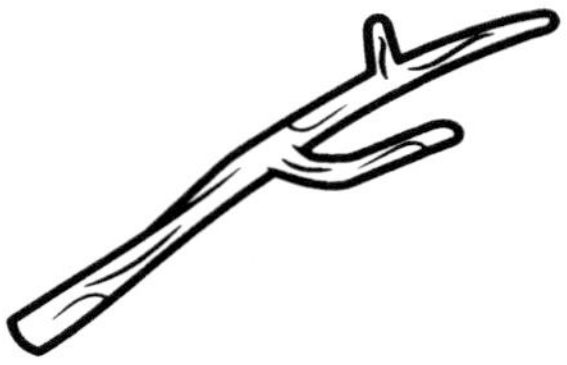

**Directions:** Use the words above that end in **-ig** and **-in** to complete the sentences.

**1.** The trash ______________________ is full.

**2.** There is a ______________________ in the wig.

**3.** I see a ______________________ in the water.

Name: ______________________

**Directions:** Use the word wheels to make words for the **-ip** and **-it** word families. Write the words on the lines. Then read the words in each word family. The first ones have been done for you.

**-ip**

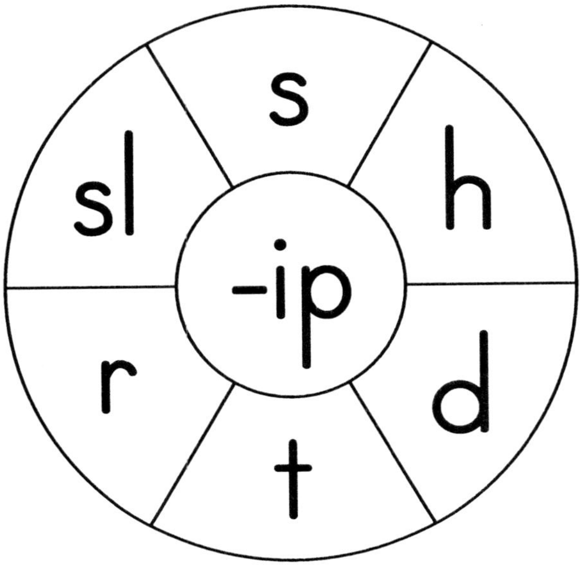


sip ______________

______________ ______________

______________ ______________

**-it**

pit ______________

______________ ______________

______________ ______________

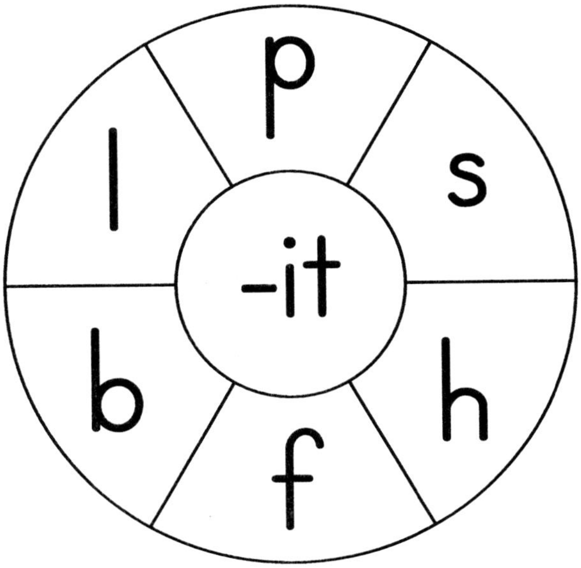

Practice 17
*Short O Word Families*
*-og & -op*

Name: ____________________________________________

**Directions:** Draw lines to match each **-og** and **-op** word to its picture.

dog frog hog hop

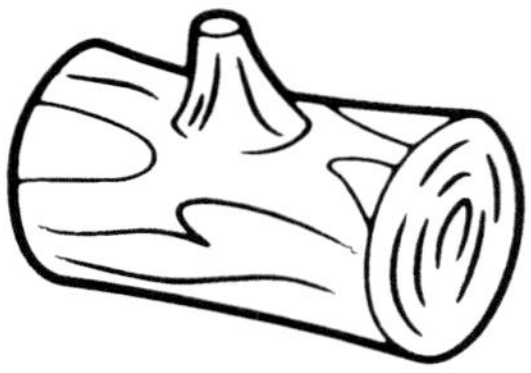

log mop chop top

**Directions:** Write the **-og** and **-op** words above in the correct section below. Then read the words in each word family.

| **-og** | | **-op** | |
|---|---|---|---|
| ______________ | ______________ | ______________ | ______________ |
| ______________ | ______________ | ______________ | ______________ |

Name: ______________________________

**Directions:** Name each picture and write the correct word family ending, **-ot** or **-ox**. Then count how many words there are in each word family and write the numbers in the boxes.

**-ot words** ☐ **-ox words** ☐

c______

f______

b______

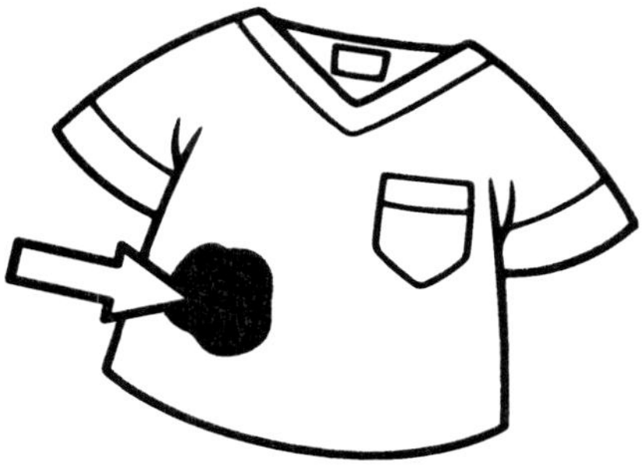

sp______

h______

p______

**Directions:** Use the **-ot** or **-ox** words from above to complete each sentence.

**1.** There is a ______________________ in the box!

**2.** We like to go in the water when it is ______________.

**Practice 19**

*Short U Word Families*
*-ub and -ug*

Name: ______________________________

**Directions:** Read each **-ub** and **-ug** word and write it beside its picture. Then read the words in each word family and listen to the matching endings.

| | | | | | | | |
|---|---|---|---|---|---|---|---|
| cub | club | hug | mug | plug | rug | sub | tub |

| -ub | -ug |
|---|---|
| 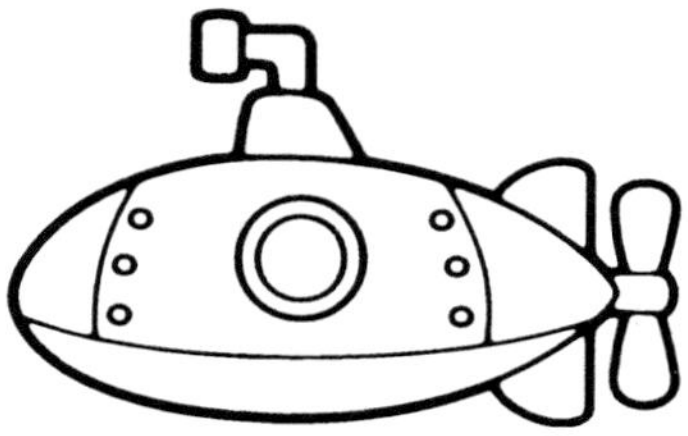 ______________ |  ______________ |
|  ______________ | 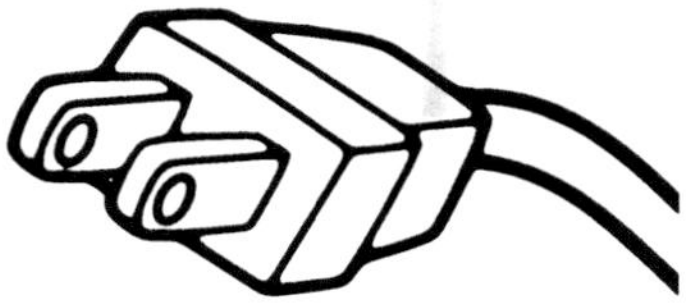 ______________ |
|  ______________ |  ______________ |
| 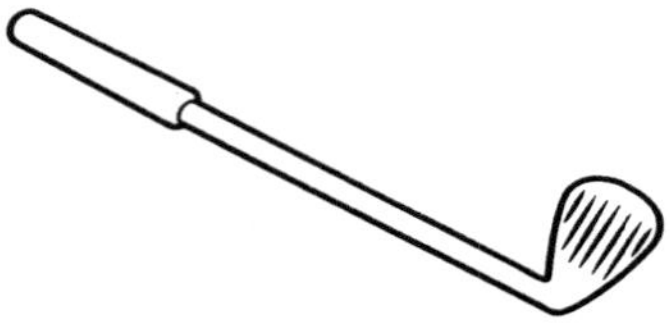 ______________ | 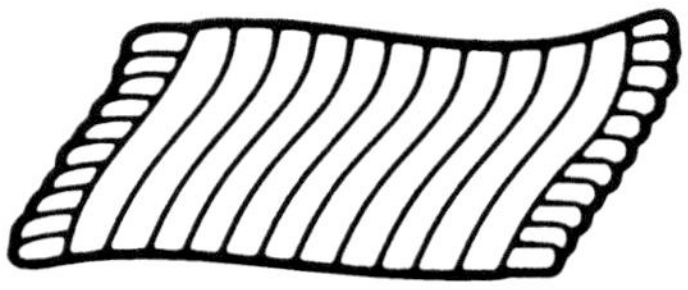 ______________ |

**Directions:** Use the words above that end in **-ub** and **-ug** to complete the sentences.

**1.** The ______________ is in the ______________!

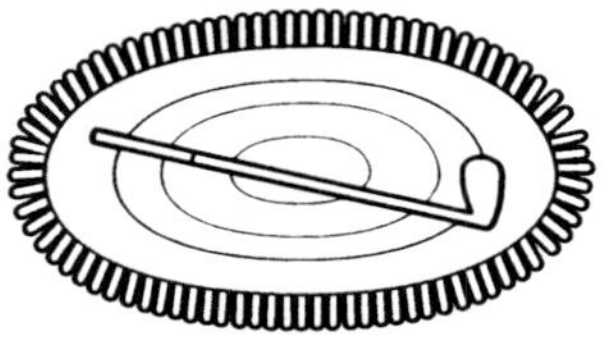

**2.** Dad's ______________ was on the ______________.

Name: ____________________________________________

**Directions:** Use the word wheels to make words for the **-un** and **-ut** word families. Write the words on the lines, and read the words in each word family. The first ones have been done for you.

**-un**

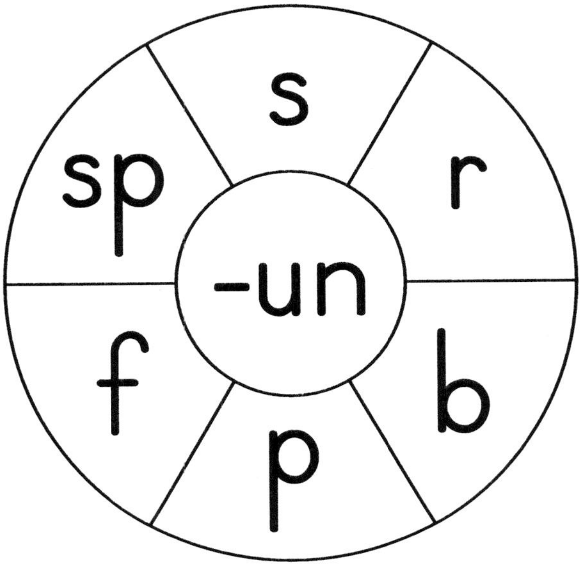


sun ____________

____________ ____________

____________ ____________

**-ut**

but ____________

____________ ____________

____________ ____________

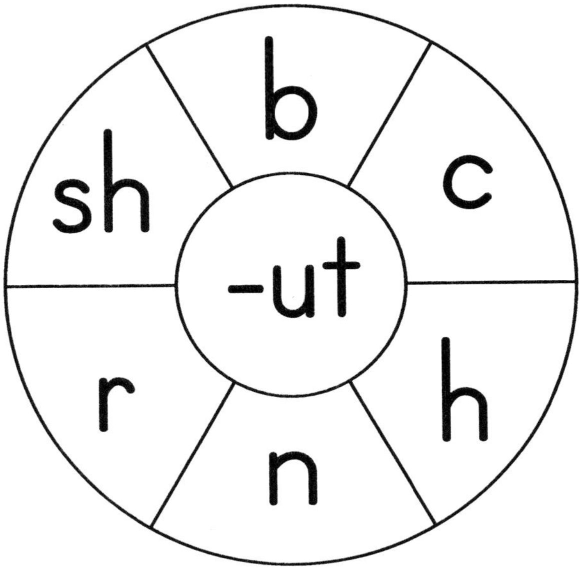

**Practice 21**
*Long A Sound*
*Silent E*

Name: ______________________________

**Directions:** The **silent e** tells the first vowel to say its name. Add the **silent e** to the letters below. Then read each word with the **long a** sound. Draw a line to match each new word to its picture.

tap___

vas___

lak___

gat___

cak___

cag___

rak___

Name: ______________________________

**Directions:** Read each **long a** word and circle the **silent e**. Write the word that best fills in each blank to complete the sentences. Read each sentence.

| | | |
|---|---|---|
| ate | face | make |
| same | skate | wake |

**1.** We can ____________________ him up now.

**2.** We will ____________________ a cake for his mom.

**3.** We each have the ____________________ hat.

**4.** We like to ____________________ on the ice.

**5.** She has a smile on her ____________________.

**6.** He ____________________ so many grapes.

**Practice 23**
*Long E Sound*
*–ee*

Name: ______________________________

**Directions:** The letters **-ee** work together to make the **long e** sound. Write the letters **-ee** in each blank and read the words.

b________

________l

j________p

**Directions:** Circle the correct **-ee** word to finish each sentence. Write the word on the line.

1. Look at that big ____________________.
   **weed** **week**

2. Did you see her ________________ out from the tree?
   **peel** **peek**

3. I need to ____________________ the dog.
   **deed** **feed**

4. I ______________________ hot in the sun.
   **feet** **feel**

**Directions:** Write **-ee** to finish each word. Read the sentences and complete each task.

| Draw a s________d. | Draw a tr________. | Draw a b________. |
|---|---|---|

Name: ______________________________

**Directions:** The letters **-ea** work together to make the **long e** sound. Write the letters **-ea** in each blank. Then read the words with the **long e** sound.

| | | | |
|---|---|---|---|
|  t________ |  s________l |  r________d | 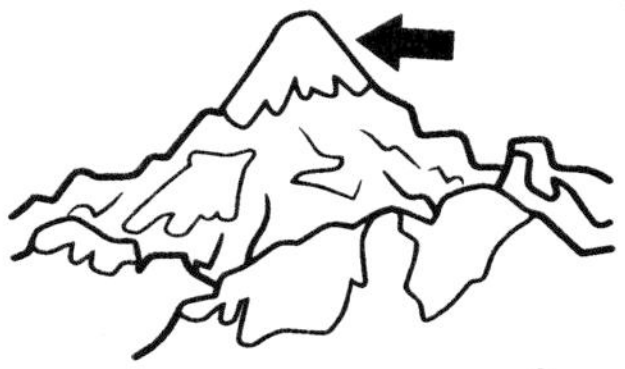 p________k |
|  st______m |  m________l |  l________f |  s________t |

**Directions:** Add **-ea** to each word and use the words to complete the sentences below. Read each sentence.

m________l   t________m   r________d

**1.** My ____________________ could not beat yours.

**2.** My dad can ____________________ that book.

**3.** It is time to eat a ____________________.

Name: ______________________________

**Directions:** Fill in the blanks below with the letter **i**. Read the words with the **long i** sound.

m___ce

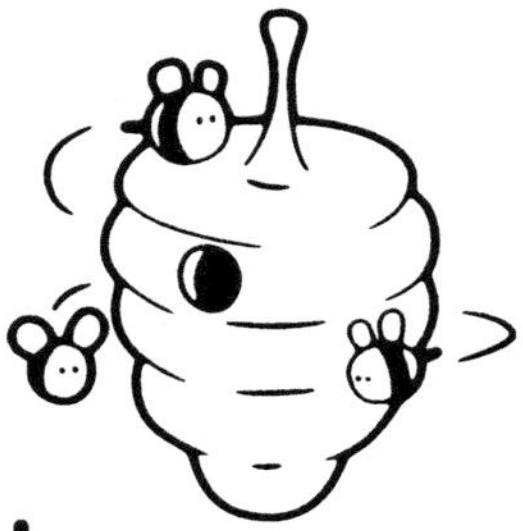

h___ve

d___ce

v___ne

b___ke

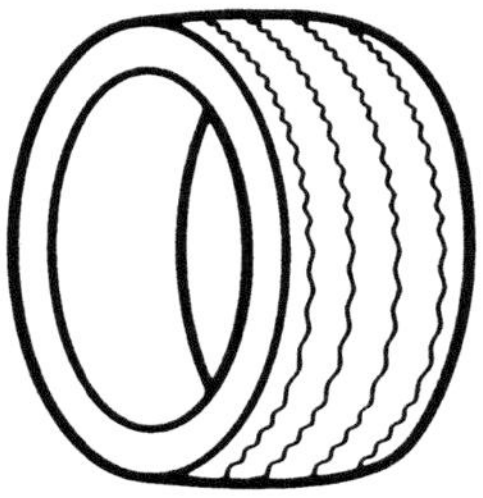

t___re

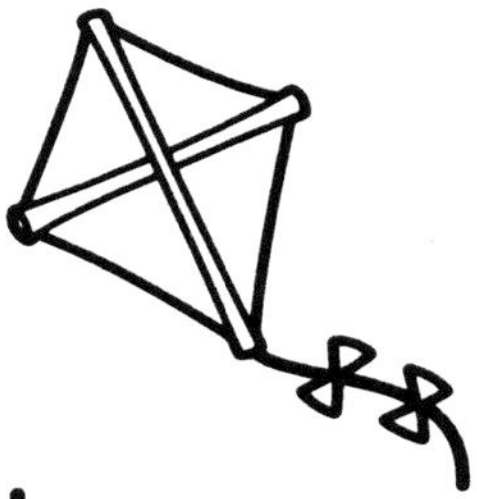

k___te

f___ve

**Directions:** Use **long i** words from above to complete each sentence below.

1. She will get a new ____________________ from her mom and dad.

2. How many ____________ are in the ____________?

3. There are ______________ ______________.

Name: ______________________________________________

**Directions:** Sometimes, the letter **y** makes the **long i** sound. Add a **y** to the end of each word and read the word. Do you hear the **long i** sound?

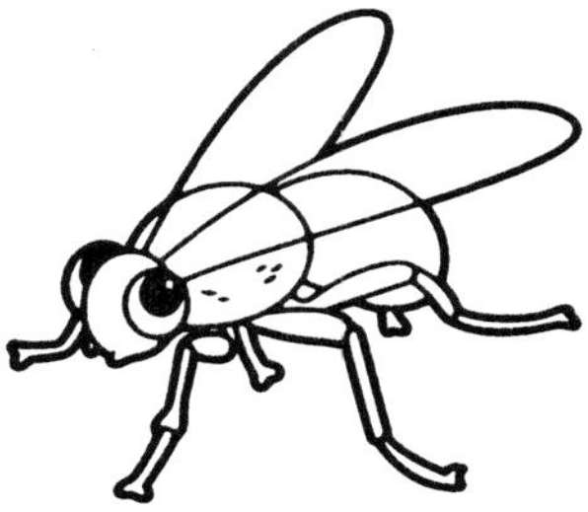
fl____

sh____

fr____

dr____

**Directions:** Use the word wheel below to make words where the letter **y** makes the **long i** sound. Then use some of the words to complete the sentences below.

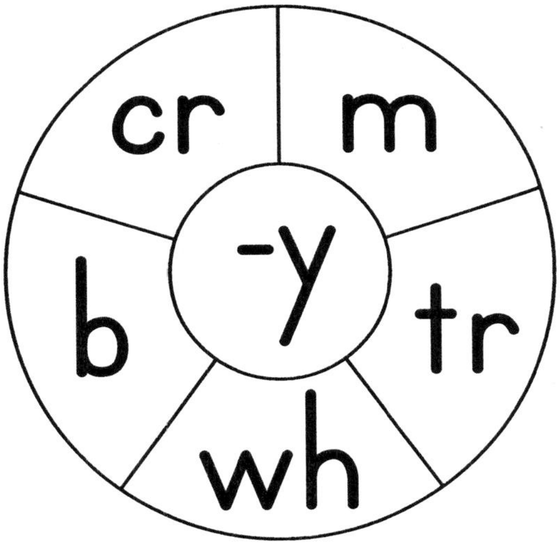


____________________ ____________________

____________________ ____________________

____________________

**1.** Dad said he would bake ____________________ cake.

**2.** They will ____________________ to fly.

**3.** What made her ____________________?

Name: ______________________________

**Directions:** Add the letter **o** to the letters below to make words with the **long o** sound. Read the words with the **long o** sound. Circle the **silent e** in each word.

r____pe

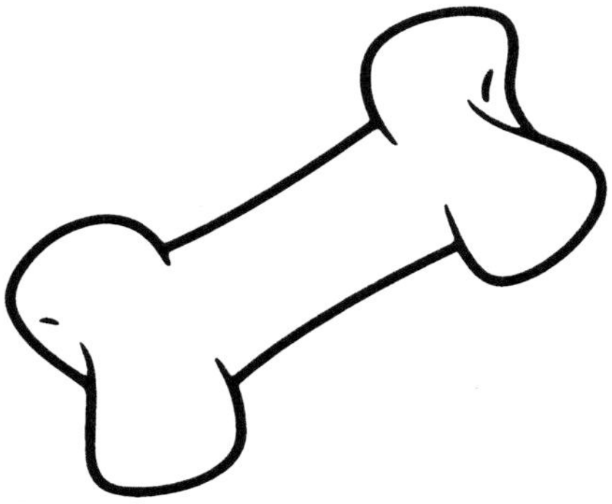

b____ne

h____se

h____me

r____be

n____te

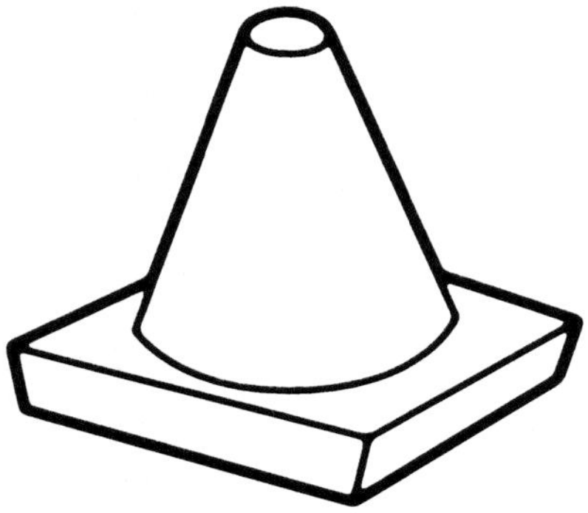

c____ne

h____le

n____se

Name: ______________________________

**Directions:** Read each sentence. Circle the words with the **long o** sound. Then write the **long o** words on the lines below each sentence.

1. There is a mole in the hole!

______________________ ______________________

2. I hope to get a blue robe.

______________________ ______________________

3. We rode in the bike zone.

______________________ ______________________

4. Smell the rose with your nose.

______________________ ______________________

5. Give them the rope and the hose.

______________________ ______________________

**Practice 29**
*Long U Sound*
*Silent E*

Name: ______________________________

**Directions:** Fill in the blanks below with the letter **u** to make words with the **long u** sound. Read the words and draw lines to match each word to its picture.

t___be

d___ne

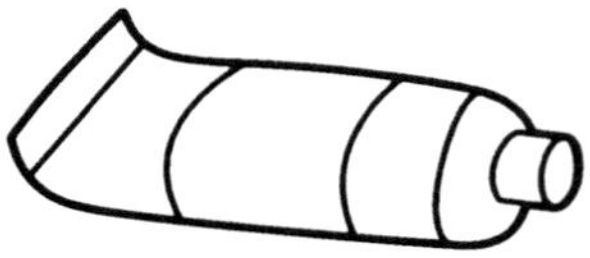

J___ne

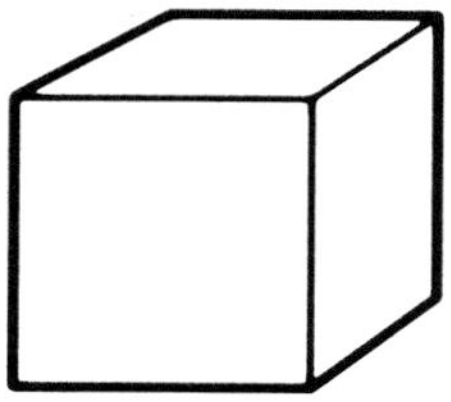

m___le

c___be

t___ne

**Directions:** Add the **silent e** to the letters below to make words with the **long u** sound. Read each word and listen to the **long u** sound.

rud___ cut___ mut___ rul___

 *©Teacher Created Resources*

Name: ____________________________________________

**Directions:** Some words make the **long u** sound when the **u** comes before the letter **i**. Fill in the blanks below with the letter **u**. Read each **long u** word.

j____ice

fr____it

s____it

**Directions:** Write the correct **long u** word listed below to finish each sentence.

clue   cute   flute   fruit   glue   juice

**1.** Sue will ____________________ the leaf to the jar.

**2.** Lulu will play a tune on her ____________________.

**3.** That puppy is so ____________________!

**4.** He drank the ____________________ after the game.

**5.** Mom said to eat more ____________________.

**6.** Did you find a ____________________?

©Teacher Created Resources

Name: ____________________________________________

**Directions:** Name each picture and listen to the beginning sounds. Add **br-** or **cr-** to the letters to complete each word.

______ush

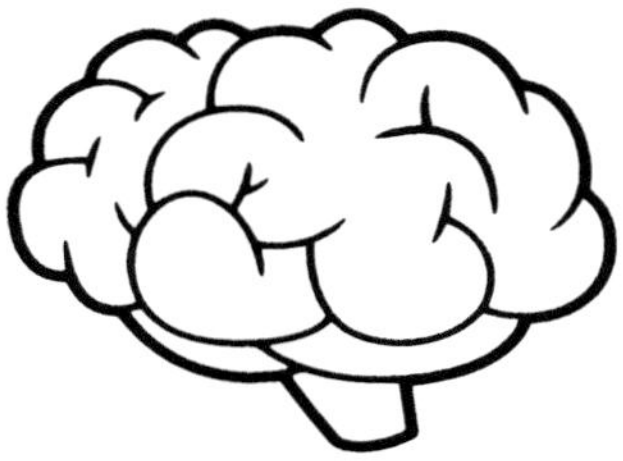

______ain

______ab

______own

______acker

______oom

______anch

______ib

______ow

______ead

______ide

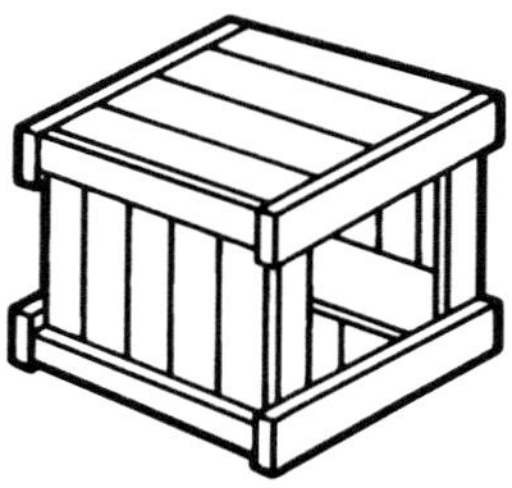

______ate

**Practice 32**
*Consonant Blends*
*dr– & fr–*

Name: ______________________________

**Directions:** Name each picture. Color the pictures that begin with the **dr- consonant blend**.

**Directions:** Use the words with the **fr- consonant blend** to complete the sentences. Read each completed sentence.

frame    frog    fruit    fry

**1.** I would like to ____________________ an egg.

**2.** The green ____________________ is in the water.

**3.** Drake's picture is in a ____________________.

**4.** Look! I made a pie with the ________________.

**Practice 33**
*Consonant Blends*
*gr– & tr–*

Name: ______________________________

**Directions:** Name each picture and listen to the beginning sounds. Add **gr-** or **tr-** to the letters to complete each word. Read the words. Then count the words with each consonant blend and write the numbers in the boxes.

**gr- blends** ☐ **tr- blends** ☐

____ash

____apes

____ee

____in

____ain

____ill

____ow

____unk

____uck

Name: ______________________________

**Directions:** Add the **bl- consonant blend** to complete each word. Read the words.

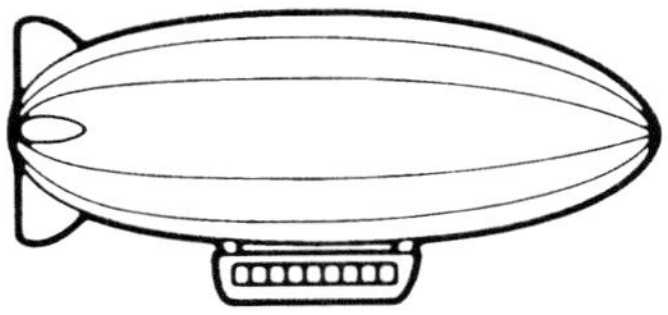

____imp

____ow

____ocks

____ade

**Directions:** Add the **cl- consonant blend** to complete each word. Then read each word and draw a line to its picture.

____ap

____ip

____ock

____ub

____am

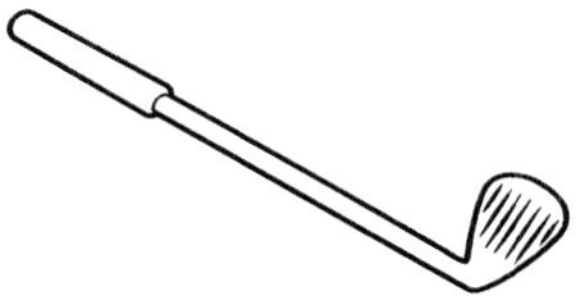

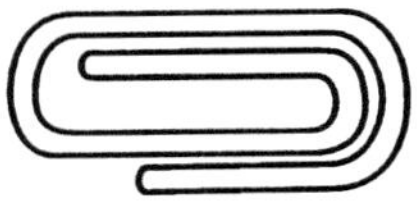

**Practice 35**

*Consonant Blends*
*fl– & gl–*

Name: ____________________

**Directions:** Name each picture. Color the pictures that begin with the **fl- consonant blend**.

**Directions:** Read the words with the **gl- consonant blend** and use them to complete the sentences. Read each completed sentence.

glass glad glue glove

1. The vase is made of ____________________.

2. I can fix the mug with ____________________.

3. I found my ____________________ in the car.

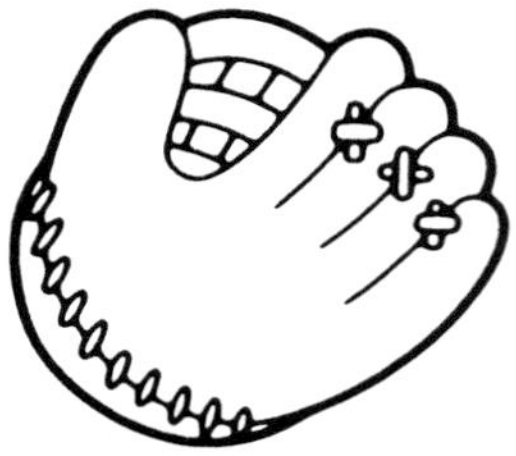

4. I was ____________________ my dad saw me play.


©Teacher Created Resources

Name: ____________________________________________

**Directions:** Name each picture and listen to the beginning sound. Add the **pl- consonant blend** or **sl- consonant blend** to complete each word. Then count the **pl- blends** and the **sl- blends** and write the numbers in the boxes.

**pl- blends** ☐ **sl- blends** ☐

_____ate

_____ug

_____ide

_____ant

_____eeve

_____eep

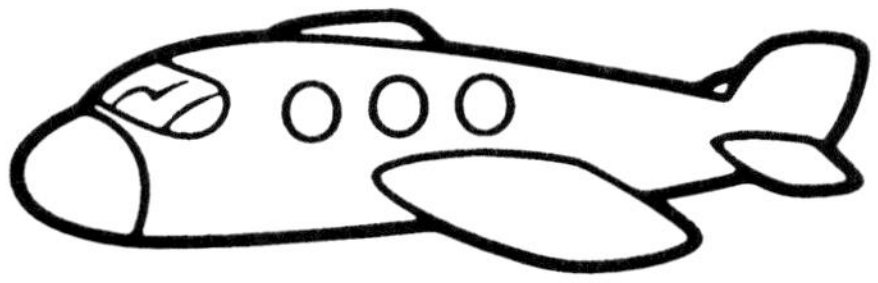

_____ane

_____ice

_____ed

Name: ________________________________

**Directions:** Add **sn-** to the letters. Then read each word with the **sn- consonant blend**.

_______ail _______ip _______ake _______ow

**Directions:** Add the **sk- consonant blend** to the letters below. Then read each word.

_______ate _______ull _______ip

_______irt _______unk _______y

Do you know how to **skip**? **yes** **no**

Do you know how to **ski**? **yes** **no**

 ©Teacher Created Resources

Name: ______________________________

**Directions:** Circle the consonant blend that fits the beginning sound for each word. Fill in the blank with the **sm-** or **st-** blend to complete the word. Read the words.

**sm** **st**

______em

**sm** **st**

______ar

**sm** **st**

______oke

**sm** **st**

______ove

**sm** **st**

______amp

**sm** **st**

______ile

**sm** **st**

______ell

**sm** **st**

______ool

**sm** **st**

______ore

Name: ______________________________

**Directions:** Name each picture. Color the pictures that begin with the **sw- consonant blend**.

**Directions:** Use words with the **sp- consonant blend** to complete the sentences. Read each sentence.

spider spin spoon spot

**1.** The ______________________ made a web.

**2.** There is a ______________________ on my shirt.

**3.** I use a ______________________ to eat my soup.

**4.** This top will ______________________ fast.

 *©Teacher Created Resources*

**Practice 40**

*Consonant Digraph*
*ch–*

Name: ______________________________

**Directions:** Add **ch-** on the lines under each picture. Read the words with the "ch" sound.

______ain

______air

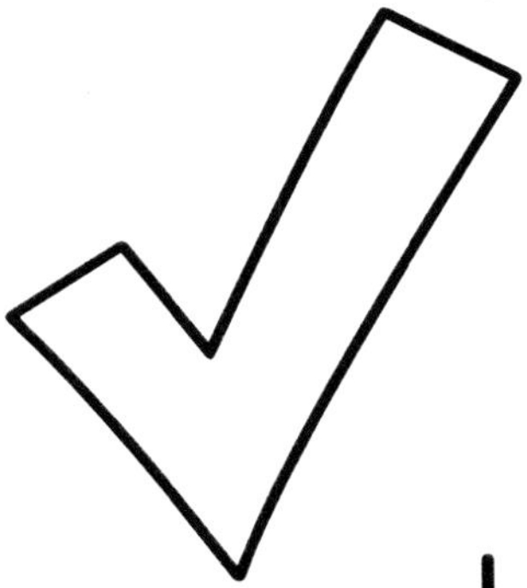

______eck

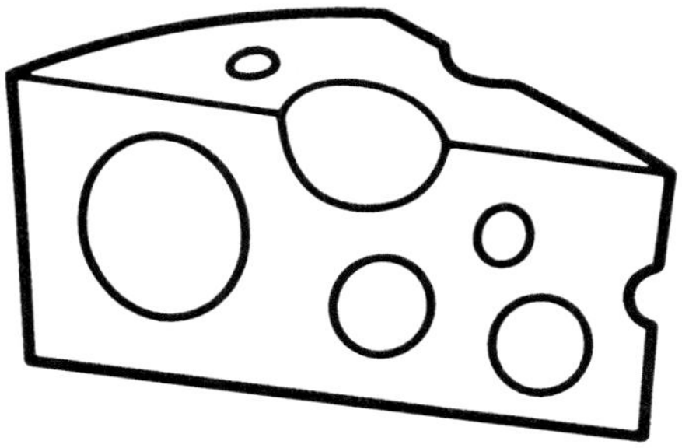

______eese

______est

______ick

______in

______ess

______op

**Practice 41**
*Consonant Digraph sh–*

Name: ______________________________

**Directions:** Add **sh-** to the beginning of each group of letters. Then read each word that makes the "sh" sound. Draw a line to connect each word to the correct picture.

______ip

______ark

______ell

______eep

______irt

**Directions:** Use a word from above to complete each sentence below.

**1.** I spilled juice on my ______________________.

**2.** All the ______________________ live on the farm.

**3.** This ______________________ is for you from me!

**4.** People said they saw a ______________________!

Name: ____________________________________________

**Directions:** Use the word wheel to make words that begin with **th-**. Write each word under its picture. Read the words that make the "th" sound.

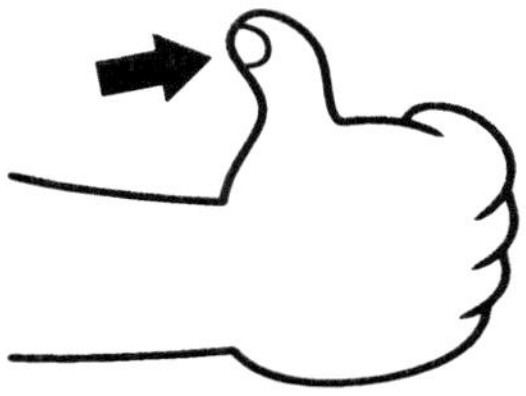

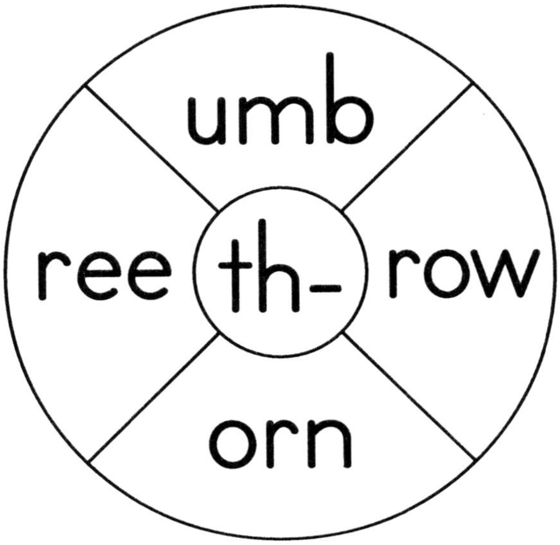


______________________  ______________________

______________________  ______________________

**Directions:** Read the **th-** words and use them all to complete the sentences below.

| | | | | | |
|---|---|---|---|---|---|
| thank | thorn | thumb | thick | thin | think |

**1.** My mom will ______________________ about it.

**2.** He gave me a hug to ______________________ me.

**3.** She got a ________________ in her ________________.

**4.** Some books are ________________ and some are ________________.

**Practice 43**

*Consonant Digraph wh–*

Name: ____________________________________________

**Directions:** Name each picture. Color the pictures that begin with the "wh" sound.

**Directions:** Add **wh** to the letters to make them into question words. Read the words.

______en ______y ______ere

______at ______ich

Name a color that begins with the "wh" sound. ____________________________

# Answer Key

**page 4**

*Color:* ball, bird, balloon, book, butterfly, bananas, bone

| | | | |
|---|---|---|---|
| cat | cow | cup | can |

**page 5**

| | | | |
|---|---|---|---|
| desk | fan | dog | dip |
| dig | fish | frog | fox |

1. fish
2. desk
3. dog, dig
4. frog, fan

**page 6**

*Color:* gate, gas, gum, glasses, goose, grapes

| | | | |
|---|---|---|---|
| hat | hill | hand | home |

**page 7**

| | | | |
|---|---|---|---|
| jet | key | jug | kite |
| jar | jump | king | kick |

1. jar 2. kick 3. king, key

**page 8**

*Color:* lemon, leg, log, lion, lamp, leaf

| | | | |
|---|---|---|---|
| mop | mitt | mug | map |

**page 9**

| | | | |
|---|---|---|---|
| pig | nail | plum | nine |
| pin | nest | nut | pen |

1. nest 2. plum 3. pig 4. nine

**page 10**

*Color:* queen, quarter, quilt, question mark, quail

rake, rug, ring, ram

**page 11**

| | | | |
|---|---|---|---|
| six | tape | sun | ten |
| star | truck | sock | tent |

1. truck 2. tent 3. star

**page 12**

*Color:* vase, violin, van, volcano, vest, vine

| | | | |
|---|---|---|---|
| web | well | watch | window |

**page 13**

| | | | |
|---|---|---|---|
| zebra | yarn | yell | zip |
| zoo | yak | zero | yo-yo |

1. yarn 2. zip 3. zero

**page 14**

*-am:* ham, jam, ram

*-ap:* cap, map, nap

1. jam, ham 2. ram 3. map

**page 15**

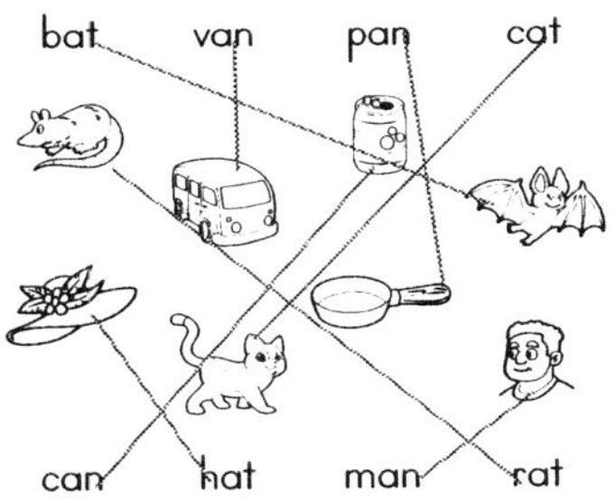


*-an:* van, pan, can, man

*-at:* bat, cat, rat, hat

**page 16**

*-et:* get, set, yet, net, let, wet

*-en:* ten, pen, hen, when, men, den

**page 17**

*-est words:* 4 *-ell words:* 5

| | | |
|---|---|---|
| bell | nest | yell |
| well | shell | vest |
| smell | test | rest |

**page 18**

| | | | |
|---|---|---|---|
| chin (blue) | fin (blue) | grin (blue) | pig (red) |
| pin (blue) | twig (red) | wig (red) | bin (blue) |

1. bin 2. twig 3. fin

**page 19**

*-ip:* sip, hip, dip, tip, rip, slip

*-it:* pit, sit, hit, fit, bit, lit

**page 20**

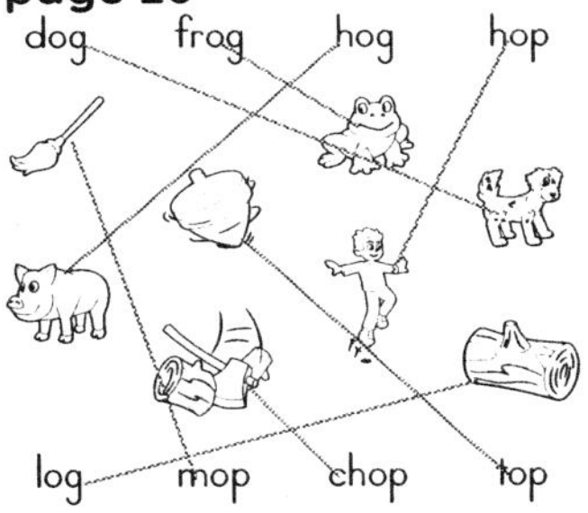


*-og:* frog, dog, hog, log

*-op:* hop, mop, chop, top

**page 21**

*-ot words:* 4 *-ox words:* 2

| | | |
|---|---|---|
| cot | fox | box |
| spot | hot | pot |

1. fox 2. hot

**page 22**

*-ub:* sub, tub, cub, club

*-ug:* mug, plug, hug, rug

1. cub, tub 2. club, rug

**page 23**

*-un:* sun, run, bun, pun, fun, spun

*-ut:* but, cut, hut, nut, rut, shut

**page 24**

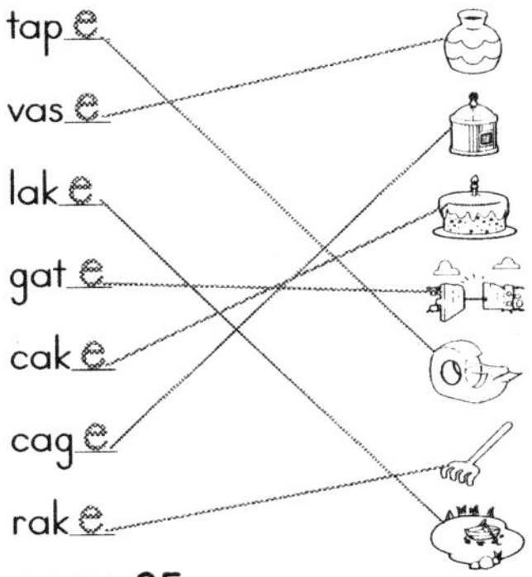


**page 25**

1. wake
2. make
3. same
4. skate
5. face
6. ate

**page 26**

| | | |
|---|---|---|
| bee | eel | jeep |

1. weed 2. peek 3. feed 4. feel

| | | |
|---|---|---|
| seed | tree | bee |

# Answer Key (cont.)

**page 27**
tea seal read peak
steam meal leaf seat
meal team read
1. team 2. read 3. meal

**page 28**
mice hive dice vine
bike tire kite five
1. bike 2. mice, tire 3. five, dice

**page 29**
fly shy fry dry
*-y:* cry, my, try, why, by
1. my 2. try 3. cry

**page 30**
Circle the e at the end of each word.
rope bone hose
home robe note
cone hole nose

**page 31**
1. mole, hole 3. rode, zone 5. rope, hose
2. hope, robe 4. rose, nose

**page 32**

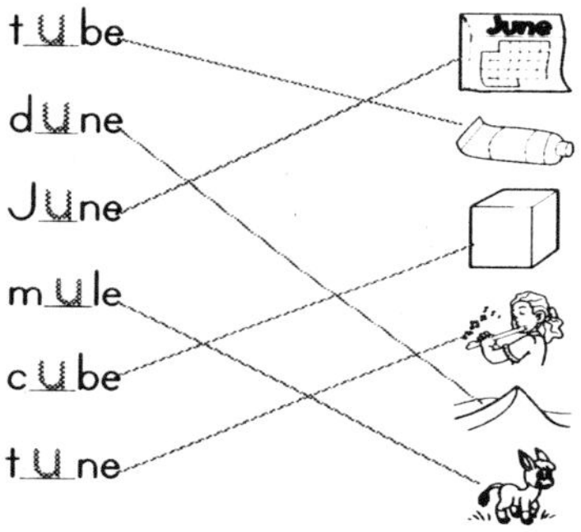


rude cute mute rule

**page 33**
juice fruit suit
1. glue 3. cute 5. fruit
2. flute 4. juice 6. clue

**page 34**
brush branch
brain crib
crab crow
crown bread
cracker bride
broom crate

**page 35**
*Color:* dress, drill, drum, dragon
1. fry 2. frog 3. frame 4. fruit

**page 36**
*gr- blends:* 4 *tr- blends:* 5
trash grapes tree
grin train grill
grow trunk truck

**page 37**
blimp, blow, blocks, blade

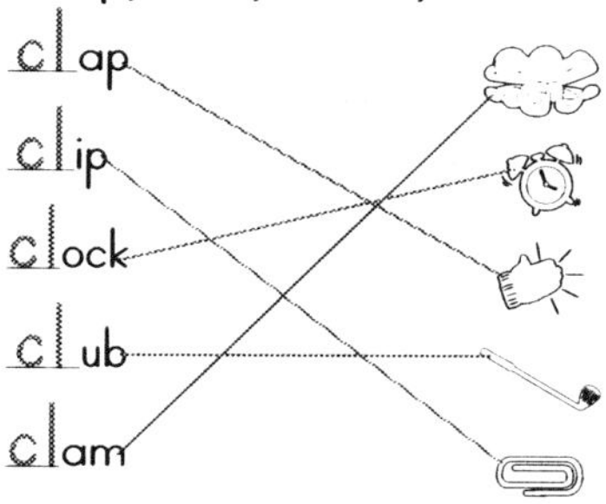


**page 38**
*Color:* flute, flamingo, flower, fly, flag
1. glass 2. glue 3. glove 4. glad

**page 39**
*pl- blends:* 4 *sl- blends:* 5
plate plug slide
plant sleeve sleep
plane slice sled

**page 40**
snail snip snake snow
skate skull skip
skirt skunk sky

**page 41**
Check that the correct blend is circled in each box.
stem star smoke
stove stamp smile
smell stool store

**page 42**
*Color:* swim, swing, swan, sweep
1. spider 2. spot 3. spoon 4. spin

**page 43**
chain chair check
cheese chest chick
chin chess chop

**page 44**

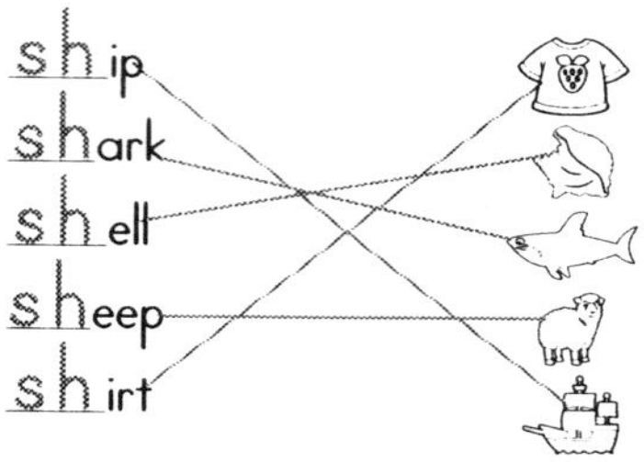


1. shirt 2. sheep 3. shell 4. shark

**page 45**
*th- :* thumb, throw, thorn, three
1. think 3. thorn, thumb
2. thank 4. thick, thin

**page 46**
*Color:* whistle, wheat, whisper, whale, wheelchair, wheel
when why where
what which
*White* is a color that begins with *wh.*